NOTHING

Lulu Raczka

NOTHING

with additional material by the Company

OBERON BOOKS
LONDON

WWW.OBERONBOOKS.COM

First published in 2014 by Oberon Books Ltd
521 Caledonian Road, London N7 9RH
Tel: +44 (0) 20 7607 3637 / Fax: +44 (0) 20 7607 3629
e-mail: info@oberonbooks.com
www.oberonbooks.com

A catalogue record for this book is available from the British
Library.

PB ISBN: 9781783191932
E ISBN: 9781783196920

Cover design by Thomas Swann

Printed and bound by Marston Book Services, Didcot.
eBook conversion by CPI Group (UK) Ltd, Croydon, CR0 4YY.

Original Production by Barrel Organ Theatre.

9 May-14 May 2013
University of Warwick Campus and Leamington Spa.

12-18 April 2014
National Student Drama Festival, Scarborough

2-17 August 2014
The Old Lab, Summerhall, Edinburgh Festival

4 October 2014
Lyric Hammersmith as part of All Change Festival

29 October 2014
Warwick Arts Centre, as part of Emerge Festival

19-22 November 2014
Camden People's Theatre

The Company:

Joe Boylan
Bryony Davies
Rosie Gray
Dan Hutton
Euan Kitson
Kieran Lucas
Jack Morning-Newton
Jack Perkins
Ali Pidsley
Lulu Raczka
Katherine Thorogood

Early Performances:

3-4 March 2013
Extract performed as part of 'Fascism, Anyone?' with the
Institute of Advanced Teaching and Learning

8 April 2013
Extract Performed at LineUp with Vertical Line Theatre.

Characters

BFF – F

Commuter – M/F (Adjustment needed when F)

Patient – M

Vandal – F

Stalker – F/M (Adjustment needed when M)

Film-Lover – M

Porn Girl – F

Nobody – M/F

Performance Notes:
These pieces are not set. The words should not
change but the pieces can be performed in any
order, by any number of people, in any space,
at any time. They can be cut and pasted in any
way you would like.
Have fun.

These are the 'Rules' used in the original
production
by Barrel Organ Theatre.
In this production the actors performed the
monologues in an improvised order and cut
for each performance. It happened in a variety
of locations, from theatrical spaces to deserted
car parks. It was completely different for every
performance.

The Rules
Start when you want.
Speak when you want.
Stand where you want.
Move where you want.
You are an audience member until you start
speaking.
Tell your story – it is your duty to make sure it is
heard.
No more than 4 stories happening at once.

Don't plan – just do.
If there is a tone developing, play against it.
The arc of the show is more important
than any individual performance.
Respond to people's actions – not to anyone's
story.
Don't look at the person who interrupts you.
Be a team – if someone is struggling, help them out
and interrupt.

Hit your marks and get out the crucial aspects of
your story – let others hit theirs.

Take risks.
Interact with the space around you.
The show does not exist in an imaginary world –
it exists in the room, in the moment.
Only 1 performer can leave during the
performance.
They can re-enter if they wish.
The audience ears are fresh, don't be afraid to
recap + repeat.
The audience should be able to talk – not share.
The audience can influence, but cannot break
this show,
let them know this if necessary.

**The audience are necessary. Don't alienate
them.**
The show is not finished.

BFF: You know Berlin doesn't have any CCTV?
    I just heard that –
    I don't even know if it's true –
    Some guy told me.
    He's probably talking shit.
    But –
    I mean –
    If it's true –
    I just don't get why?
    I mean –
    CCTV is there to protect people –
    It's there –
    You know –
    So that people know they're being watched –
    That they can't just do what they want –
    It's important.
    I get that it doesn't always work.
    I mean –
    Look at what happ –
    But still –
    It's –

    I told her to text me when she got home.
    I mean –
    We always do that –
    You know –
    It's what they tell you to do at school –
    And on TV and whatever –
    I just went to sleep
    She never text me –
    But I was asleep anyway –
    So I guess –

    She doesn't really talk about it –
    Well –
    Sometimes –

I dunno –
Once in a while I get a phone call and she's on the other
end in tears and I just –
I dunno –
Freeze up –
Cause what can I actually say to her?
I don't understand what she's going through –
How can I?
I can give her fuck all –
I –

She used to be so fun –
I know I would say that –
Cause –
Obviously –
She's my friend –
Why would I be friends with her if she wasn't fun?
But actually –
To be honest –
I have loads of fucking boring friends –
She was so funny too –
But also –
She was really hot –
Cause usually girls –
They're either hot or they're funny –
Like –
You know –
They're not both –
Cause if you're always hot –
Why do you need to be funny?
Everyone is always gonna like you –

I tried to call her in the morning –
But there was no answer –
I didn't even think anything of it –
I just waited for her to call me back –

We decided that she was the only one of our friends who
could pull off a click –
You know what I mean?
Like a sassy girl click?
Obviously she wouldn't –
But if she did it wouldn't be lame –
OK –
Well –
It would still be lame –
But she could have done it way better than any of us –
Not that I would –
You know –

This guy dumped her really harshly –
And seriously –
I don't know why cause he was fucking hideous –
A week later he turned up to a party with some other girl –
And I mean –
She wasn't even hot –
Like not at all –
And we were all like –
Do a sassy girl click!
Do a sassy girl click!
Do a sassy girl click in her face!
And she wouldn't
Cause –
Obviously –
That would be weird

I keep thinking though –
What if this happened to me?
Cause it happens all the time
And now –
Every time I walk home –
I just think –
Is this gonna be my moment?

Is it gonna happen tonight?
Like –
As if like –
It's definitely going to happen –
And I think –
What am I wearing now?
And sometimes I think that I'm fucking crazy –
And then I think that I'm just being sensible –
Cause –
You know –
It does happen a lot –
And then I think that crazy people think they're just being sensible –
So yeah –
But it does happen all the time –

He cut off all her hair.
Her mum didn't say that on the phone –
So when I went to see her I didn't know what to do –
Should I mention it?
It was just like this giant elephant in the room
She looked so awful –
And I just sat there –
Cause –

She went home early that night –
I usually walk with her –
But not that night –
She'd got into such a fight with this girl –
Basically –
She's got with this guy that one of our friends had been kinda dating –
Not properly or anything –
I don't even think he liked her –
Beth gave him head or whatever –
And the other girl was really annoyed –

I mean –
Let's face it –
Obviously –
But she is proper frigid –
So –
In the end –
I just thought –
If you're not gonna give your boyfriend head –
And he wasn't even her boyfriend anyway –
But if you're not gonna give your boyfriend head –
He's probably gonna get it off another girl –
And I know that's really harsh –
And like –
It's not like I give guys head all the time or anything –
But that's just what guys are like –
You know?
So she left early –
Cause everyone was annoyed with her –
And the guy –
The guy she gave head to –
He just –
Well whatever –
He's such a wanker

They haven't caught the guy –
The guy who

I hope they do –
I want him to go to prison

Like –
I really want him to go to prison –
I think about it quite a lot –
Him –
In prison –

Not in a weird way –
I guess it is weird though –
I want him in one of those shower rooms –
Those big ones –
That you see in those films –
All white –
And –
I want him alone –
In just this big white room thing –
Then –
Right –
Some hand –
A big hand –
Strong –
It grabs him –
Right round the neck and the guy –
The guy with the hand –
Throws him to the floor –
On all fours –
Like a fucking dog –
He squeals –
But he knows what's coming –
So he shuts the fuck up –
Cause he doesn't want anyone to come in and see this –
He just waits and then it comes –
Big and hard –
Into his tiny –
Virginal little arsehole –
The force knocks him to the ground –
It's so fucking hard it's breaking the skin –
It's actually drawing blood –
I just think about it going in and out –
And in and out –
And with every thrust he gulps down another scream –
With one final whack the guy cums –
Like it was nothing –

He feels the blood and semen trickle down his crack –
He starts to cry and the guy just licks the tears away –

COMMUTER:

Note for Female Performer:
The 'girlfriend' at the beginning remains the 'girlfriend', but they are now dating a new 'girl' or 'woman', not 'guy'.

Example:
'And now she's dating this other girl/woman'
'I am a woman who is able to acknowledge when another woman is attractive'.

I was on the train –
Back to the city –
And all I could think was I needed a night out –
A big one.

My ex had just started dating this new guy –
And –
Being completely honest –
This is not someone I'm 'over' –
I'm still in that stage where I think she's perfect –
I mean –
She's a bitch cause she dumped me –
But except for that detail –
Which is –
You know –
Pretty insignificant when we look at the grand scheme of things –
She's perfect.
And now she's dating this other guy who is.

OK –
Now –
I am a man who is able to acknowledge when another man is attractive –

You know –
I'm comfortable enough with myself –
To be able to say –
That this man –
Her new man –
Is yes –
Attractive –
Very fucking attractive.
They are both very attractive.

So I needed a night out –
I needed –
To be pretty fucking crude –
Some new sexual imagery –
Cause right now –
I've got her –
And it's just –
Well –
You know –
Not nice –
So this just –
Yeah.
Too much.
I needed a night out.

I get off the train –
And it's so comforting –
Among all these people –
Just so many people –
All independently going about their business –
Like –
They don't care about me –
And that's fine –
Better than fine –
I'm free –
You know?

I was fucking excited to get home.
I was properly fucking excited.
And within an hour of getting home I'm off to crash some
18th across town –

We're a bit old.
We're a lot old actually.

Fuck it.

We go to the pub –
We pick up –
Like we're the fucking teenagers –

But it's shit.
The party –
It's shit –
Really –
Truly shit –
It is an 18th –
I went into the kitchen for a drink –
Just a glass of water –
And it's packed.
Why –
Why when the music is on in the living room –
Does everyone always stand in the kitchen?
Just chatting –
In the kitchen –
Against the fucking oven –
And every few minutes someone accidentally turns it on –
And some girl freaks out about the fucking gas –
Or just outside the toilet –
You think it's a queue but it's just some guy chatting away –
Outside the fucking door –
And you're like –

Is this the queue and he's like –
What?
As if that is the most fucking insane suggestion –
And then he kind of clocks the toilet and rolls his eyes –
As if you built a fucking toilet in front of his hand to fuck
up his plan to get laid –

And I thought that this was kind of enough.

If I'd known –
But I didn't.

Grabbed my coat –
Didn't wait to say bye –
And I left –
People always say –
'I could feel something was going to happen' –
But I couldn't –
I felt like nothing was gonna happen –
I turned onto the main road –
The kebab shops aren't busy yet –
I see a pair of shoes in the window of a Topman –
And I don't usually shop in Topman –
But they looked smart –
For work –
It's funny –
Well not funny –
You know –
If I hadn't been looking I wouldn't have noticed –
See my head was turned left –
So when I carried on walking I noticed this weird shape at
the end of the alley –
If I'd been looking straight I wouldn't've seen –
When you really think about all those tiny details –
How they all add up –
If I'm being honest –

Usually –
If I saw something down some street I wouldn't do
anything about it –
If it was later –
But it was pretty early –
And I –
I don't know –
I wasn't being brave –
I was just being stupid –
Not stupid –
Just wasn't thinking –
There was this boy –

You know when you see a photo?
And the image just doesn't make sense –
The picture just doesn't look –
Doesn't look whole –
And you can't see why –
It's usually war pictures –
Usually fucked-up pictures –
And you kind of trace it –
You go –
There's the torso –
There's the shoulder –
Oh shit!
There's no hand!
That's how it looks now –
The boy looks like that now –
In my head –
Then –
Then this boy –
He looked fine –
He was –
I saw that he'd been hit or something –
His face –
It was bruised –

And then I saw –
He was –
His leg was –
It was gone –
Gone below the knee –

I don't mean that he didn't have a leg –
Well I do –
But I mean –
It wasn't an old injury –
It had been cut off.
That.
That night.
Just hacked.
Right there.
Just.
There was so much blood.
And bone.
I was standing in it.
The blood.

It fucking stank.

I couldn't touch him –
To comfort him.

The first thing that struck was just the plain practicality of
it –
How the fuck could you do that?
I don't mean ethically –
Or whatever –
But how is it physically possible –
How do you have the strength to cut through?

And I –
I just couldn't touch him –

All I needed to do was just reach out –
And I don't know –
Stroke him –
Not like a dog –
But –
Yeah –
Like the way you comfort a pet –
He was just this boy.
And I just.
I couldn't.

Opposite me there was this bill-board –
Daniel Craig –
His face –
Giant –
Grinning –
Or sneering –
I dunno just confident –
And I wanted to grab him and show him and say look –

If I could've just touched him

All this random shit was rushing through my head.
Just like random facts and stuff –
No –
Not even facts –
Just pictures –
Just rushed through –
Like how the sheep on the hillside stand slanted –

The ambulance arrived –
They said thanks for waiting –
They didn't seem suspicious –
I didn't ask anything –
I –
Why would I?

I had done what I was supposed to –
I got on the bus –
It was crowded –
It was late now –
And I –
The guy standing beside me –
I can see the skin of his wrist as he holds the bar –
There's those little hairs –
I want to tell him –
But I don't –
I mean –

You'll know that it's been in the news.
Unsurprisingly everyone is very disgusted.

I called my ex –
There was no answer –

How do you tell people this?
It's not like it happened to me –
I don't have anything to do with it –
But I am –
I am involved –
I just went home –

FILM-LOVER: I really really like films.
    I know.
    That sounds really fucking boring –
    Everybody likes films –
    But films –
    Films –
    They reaffirm my life –
    That sounds like something out of a health brochure –
    Mental health –
    Whatever –

I just mean that films make me feel better about things if
I'm sick or tired or whatever –
I don't like the serious ones –
OK –
Well some serious ones –
Just not difficult ones –
I don't like watching things that are difficult –
That art crap –
You know –
I'm watching this to feel better –
So it should make me feel better –
I know people say difficult films make you realize the
horrible shit in your life –
But I don't think so –
Anyway –
I like my life –
It's quite good –
I have things going on –

One of my friends wants to write films –
He gets really angry whenever I say this to him –
He thinks the point of film is to be challenging –
Challenge the norm –
He always says the point of film is to wake us up –
From what?
I ask –
He just gave me that look –
Like he just understood everything so much better than I did –
But I mean –
But how can he –
He's a depressive –
He's clinically depressed –
That sounds harsh –
But come on –
How well can you understand life if you're a depressive?
He says much better.

But –
Come on –

I didn't really take it seriously at first –
I dunno –
It just –
I played a prank on him –
I thought it was genius.
He didn't.
Well –
He will –
In time –
He always used to complain to me about girls and all that
shit –
And so I thought this might be the cure –
I sent him a stripper –
Dressed as a therapist –
All-in-one!
Girl and help!
I'm really annoyed I wasn't there –
Cause –
I wanted to see what a stripper's take on a therapist
costume would be –
Come on –
That would be fucking brilliant –
As you know –
He didn't think so –
He had such a go at me for not taking him seriously –
But come on –
Imagine a stripper trying to help a fucking depressive –
That's a movie –
Stripper with a heart of gold –
Cynical guy in a dressing gown –
Whiskey in a coffee mug –
Awkward slapstick at the beginning –
By the end –

They're in love –
She's back at university –
He's writing again –
That's a movie I'd watch –
He said the joke was symbolic of my entire attitude
towards life –
And I was like yes!
Yes it is!
I like having fun!

We have arguments about absolutely everything.
The worst was a few months ago.
I was talking about this company that I was selling stuff
to –
Some vague science-based thing –
Computer shit –
You know –
Boring –
Turns out they make weapons –
Not only weapons –
Still the boring computer stuff –
But some of that's weapons –
And I thought he'd find this funny –
Cause they'd been so secretive –
And it was like –
Of course they were –
They make weapons –
I don't claim to know much about any of the actual
weapon making –
But I met all these people working there –
And they invited me out with them –
And I invited him –
Cause you know –
He really needs to get out more.
And he was disgusted.
And then we had this big fight –
And I was like –

When it comes down to it –
When it fucking comes down to it –
Someone's gotta do it!
Whatever.
He wouldn't come.

So this night –
It ends up being one of those nights –
A bar –
Then a club –
Then a house –
I have no idea what their fucking house actually looked
like now –
But in my head there was a fucking jacuzzi –
Or at least one of those fridges that has an ice machine –
Anyway –
Loads of people were on something –
And I was just minding my own business –
Enjoying my fucking luck –
When some girl passed out or something –
I dunno –
I can't remember –
And some guy started getting all fucked up about it –
Then he punched this other guy –
And I just stood back and watched the carnage –
And I filmed it –
Cause why not?
It was hilarious!
I wasn't gonna do anything with it.
I sent it to Jonny –
Cause I thought I had a good tag line –
'Life imitating art' –
I meant that it looked like a scene from a movie –
Not that witty or insightful obviously –
But I was wasted so who cares –
It was funny –
He just sent back –

You're fucked up –
That was it –
I got kinda annoyed cause he –
He –
Was calling me fucked up –
So I responded –
Who's the one on anti-depressants?
He just didn't reply –
Which isn't like him –
Cause he usually enjoys telling me what a dick I am –

But like –
The thing is –
Is that I don't actually know what to say –
Cause the thing is –
I don't understand what he's going through –
You know?
He's depressed –
I'm not depressed –
He doesn't seem to get that everything is so much easier
than he's making it out –
He –
He thinks about stuff a lot –
When actually life is pretty simple –
You want money?
Get a job –
You want a girl?
Ask her out –
If you're trying to decide between your girlfriend and
another girl –
You probably like the second one more –
You know?
When I make jokes and stuff –
It's just me trying to say –
Just trying to say that if he just laughs –
He'll feel better –

I just don't understand how he feels –

I'm seeing him in hospital today.
I'm just gonna try and be nice –
And not –
You know –
Get him all riled up or anything –
I bought flowers –
I'm just trying to decide whether that's lame.

PORN GIRL: I want to talk about my relationship with porn.
I want to talk about how I started watching porn.
Cause I used to watch porn a lot.

I'm sorry.
This is fucking horrible.

I remember discovering masturbating.
And I thought it was the most exciting thing that had ever happened to me.
It was pretty fucking groundbreaking.

But then –
This was before I'd had sex.
And then I had sex.
And you know –
Sex and masturbation can't really be compared.
I was a teenager –
So let's face it –
Actual sex wasn't even that great.
But I didn't know that.
But –
The act of someone else giving you an orgasm was fucking amazing.
So –
For a while –
I didn't masturbate.

But then –
Obviously –
Me and my teenage sexual partner broke up –
Then I tried to start masturbating again.
But now there were problems.

I know I'm saying this all weirdly.
I know it sounds weird.

Firstly –
There was the problem of fantasy.
Now that I had experienced the reality –
I realized how pathetic my fantasies were.
Now that I had experienced it –
I couldn't imagine it.
I just couldn't create the kind of intimacy in my head that
you experience in real life.
So when I tried –
I just couldn't really get excited about it.

And the other problem was that I was only doing it cause I
was bored.
It was probably when I'd just started working full-time.
I was really tired –
And bored –
And I just wanted to come home and wank –
But I wasn't actually turned on –
I just wanted to do it to break up the fucking evening
before I went to bed and went to work again.
I had nothing to do really.
I was living with my mum and I felt like shit.
I just needed the time to myself.

Cause the thing is –
Right now –
I honestly can't see myself actually having sex.

I'm so.
I dunno.
The idea of me actually having sex –
The idea of anyone actually having sex with me –
The whole idea –
The very idea of me being interested in the whole thing.
I dunno –
It's ridiculous.
Cause –
To put it bluntly –
Who would fucking want to?

But then there was porn –
And it did all that for me.
I didn't have to think of myself like that.
I didn't have to think of anyone wanting me like that.

I always felt pretty disgusting afterwards though.

I also didn't like touching myself anymore.
When I was a lot younger I just used to masturbate with
my fingers or whatever –
But now.
Now that made me feel kind of gross.
It felt a bit pathetic.
Embarrassing.
So then I bought something mechanic.
That felt better.

Problem was –
After all this –
I had to accept certain things I didn't like about myself.

See –
What I liked –
What I really liked –

What really turned me on –
Was fucking horrible.
It wasn't the people kissing and liking each other that
turned me on –
It was the horrible shit.
It was the moment the guy forces a girl to go down on him –
And you can see her eyes watering.
It was that bit where the guy is fucking the girl so hard you
can pretty much hear her skin bruising –
And she is trying so hard to look like she's not in pain –
But cause of the shit cameras and lighting you can see her
flinching.
I liked it –
But I didn't like that I liked it.
I liked the bits where something felt wrong –
When it felt pushed.
And there I am –
Wanking over it.
Alone –

The thing is –
If you start –
If you start liking that stuff.
It's a hole.
I didn't know where to find it –
But I knew I could find some horrible shit if I looked for
five minutes.
Maybe longer –
If I'd tried –
I could have found some properly horrible stuff –
The kind of stuff where they're not trying to cover up the
horrible nasty shit –
Where the horrible nasty shit is the point.
I know it's out there –
There must be so much horrible shit.

But I had to stop watching it altogether.

I couldn't let myself go that far.
Now I can believe the best in myself.
I can believe that I'd have found the horrible porn –
And it wouldn't have turned me on –
That I'd have seen it –
And I'd think –
That is fucking disgusting.
The world is fucking horrible.
I pledge to spend the rest of my life trying to change it.
But I wouldn't have done that.
I would have just wanked over it and cried.

My mum decided I needed to see a therapist.
Not about the porn –
I don't speak to her about the porn.
She got bored of me moping around –
And she couldn't really get why I wasn't excited about all
of the opportunities that were available to me.
And I told her it was because there weren't any
opportunities available to me –
I told her that I couldn't think of any opportunities
available to me.
And then I said that I was putting in all of my energy –
All of my energy into something that made me sad and
tired –
Just so I could get money.
And she said that I needed money to live.
And I said that I understood the premise –
But at the moment I felt like I was throwing everything I
had into a void.
And it didn't seem like a fair exchange.
And I think she kind of agreed.
She must've agreed.
I assume she thought of this when she was my age –

Or earlier –
I'm sure everyone has this realization –
But at some point –
I guess you have to accept it and just get the fuck on with it.

To be honest –
I think I just need to hang out with my friends more.

VANDAL: So I'm very angry.
There's this guy at work.
He's a fucking asshole.
No.
But seriously –
He's actually.
I'm at work –
Which –
By the way –
At this particular moment –
Meant me standing at the entrance to this canteen at a
fucking classic car festival taking tickets.
12 hours.
I'd be taking paper tickets.
Sometimes they were blue –
Sometimes they were shiney –
But they were always fucking tickets –
And I was always fucking taking them.

It was 6 in the morning.
And you know what?
I can kind of admit –
Admit –
That this isn't my dream job –
And I know that in a recession I'm lucky to have a job –
I should just be happy I'm not feeding my twelve kids my
own shit.
But seriously.

Fuck.
This.

So this one morning,
I'm standing there.
The place is fucking empty and I'm not smiling,
I'm not smiling –
Because as I've said –
I'm not happy.
And this guy comes up to me –
And he's an asshole –
The asshole –
And he says –
You know you could smile?
He's not my fucking superior –
He's actually worked there less time than me.
And he just.
Fucking hell.
Then he was like –
You look like you're lining people up to kill them.
And I just thought –
Who??
There is no one fucking here.
But apparently –
According to wankface over there –
I am supposed to be happy –
Unconditionally.

I couldn't even contain it.
I was so fucking.

So I followed him home.
I know.
That's weird.
But I just really needed to know where he lived.
I really needed to know who he lives with –

Cause –
Who fucking likes him?
Seriously?

Then –
I woke up –
In the middle of the night –
Needing a shit.
I thought this was an odd occurrence cause I've woken up
for a piss before –
But not to shit –
That can usually wait till morning.
Not that night though!!
And I thought –
And I'm not a person who usually cares for the whims of
fate –
But then I thought –
This shit –
This shit is special –
I need to use this for something.
So I put on a coat.
Went out.
And I shat on his doorstep.
Not at the gate.
No –
I shat on his doorstep.
He even had a mat.
It was perfect.
That night I slept great –
Angst free.
So I started doing it every night.
During the day I'd pick out an offender –
And this was easy –
Because fucking hell –
So many people are assholes.
Then I would follow them home.

And I would shit on their doorstep.

Problem is –
If it's gonna fuck with them –
They need to know it's human poo.
Dog shit isn't quite the same.
So I started thinking about signs.
I bought toothpicks and pink post-its.
I made these little flags that said –
'This is human poo' –
They're just fucking adorable.
Cause they couldn't be mistaken.
They had to know that an actual human being –
Had taken down their actual trousers –
And their underwear –
And shat on their mat.
It may have taken a while.
They may have been reading a newspaper.
But don't mistake it.
They were a person.
Who shat on your doorstep.

I'd been dragged to this club for a friend's birthday.
God knows why.
I fucking hate clubbing.
I find it to be a very alienating experience –
Doesn't everybody feel that?
It kind of hits me when I'm there.
It really fucking hits me –
That every person in here is each their own individual person –
That each of these fucking people is a sentient being –
Each with their very own thoughts and brain waves.
It's like –
I mean it's fucking bleak.

There's a guy beside me.

He's dancing –
Or –
Trying to.
He's got a watch on –
It's too big for him –
It's just sliding up and down his arm as he dances –
Like –
This big hunk of metal rubbing against his skin –

And then I see that fucking prick.
The smiling asshole.
That one.
I started walking towards him.
I had an idea.

I was going to hate-fuck him.

This was a term I heard bandied around –
That I suddenly –
Very clearly –
Understood.
And –
I mean –
I had started expressing myself pretty primally in recent
times –
I could just try it –
I tapped him on the shoulder –
Which was unnecessary cause I was standing in front of
him –
But it seemed very necessary that I tap him on the
shoulder –
I whispered –
I want you to fuck me in the ass until I cry –
Clearly he didn't really feel like it –
Cause he moved away –
And then kind of laughed –

I think he was trying to work out whether I was joking –
Then he asked whether I was at work on Wednesday.
Hate-fucking wasn't working.
So I just said –
I shat on your doorstep.
Can't really explain what happened –
Cause nothing did –
He just looked at me –
So –
I repeated –
I shat on your doorstep.
Then he looked at me again and weirded out and walked away.

I pissed on the street on the way home.
I know.
I just really needed the kick of it.
I wanted to shit but I didn't need to shit.
It's really fucking hard to make yourself shit when you don't need to shit.
I mean obviously.
I needed to do it though.
So I downed a pint of tap water and pissed outside a bank.
Cause they're assholes.
I think I need to stop this whole thing.

I don't know if I can go to work anymore.
I might actually have to quit.
Fuck.
You know what?
I don't actually have any fucking clue what I can do after that.

PATIENT: My work has sent me to a therapist –
Cause –
Well –
I don't even know why –

I've really been trying recently –
I don't mean that I'm a dick usually –
Well –
No –
I kind of am.
I just tend to piss people off pretty easily just by being myself –
Sometimes I talk to people and I just think –
You are a fucking idiot.
And then I have to tell them –
Cause how else are they gonna learn?
Generally speaking people aren't happy to hear that.
Fucking obviously.
But recently –
Recently –
I've been really trying not to do that –
Cause OK –
I finally worked out that when you don't tell people that they're stupid –
They tend to like you more.
So I thought this was a better way to go about life.
Though I meet so many unbelievable retards.
Actually.
I'm sorry.
I don't like to use that word.
My mum gets annoyed when I do –
And I respect my mum.
She works hard.
Anyway –
The other week –
I just got pissed at this guy –
Cause he was –
Well –
Being an idiot.
Fucking dim.
And now.

Now I'm going to see a therapist –
To sort through my issues.
It's great –
You get angry –
Not even angry –
I wouldn't even say I was angry –
Annoyed –
You get annoyed and suddenly you are a person who has issues.

But this could be my chance to talk about stuff.
You know –
Big stuff.
OK
See –
Right –
I have this thing –
There's this little thing that happened to me –
Just –
I don't know if I should even call it a thing –
Cause it really wasn't that big a deal –
When I was a boy –
A child –
There was this man –
Family friend –
Fucking always –
And he –
You –
He –
You get it –
He.

I can't actually say the words.
I can't even think what words I would use.
It's not a thing to be described in words.

I know what it is I'm trying to describe but the actual act of describing it just seems fucking impossible.

Absolutely fucking repulsive.

I can't even remember what he looked like.

I try so hard.

Brown hair

White shirt

Black trousers

Glasses

Shoes

Pretty fucking generic.

I mean –

Am I even describing an actual person?

Or am I describing like –

The fucking clip art picture of a man?

What I can remember is how it felt.

I'm still fucking lying.

I can't really remember how it felt –

I've tried to remember –

I try to kind of re-feel it –

I just imagine hands –

And then I'm just like –

What the fuck are you doing?

Why the fuck are you actively trying to go through that again?

I mean for fuck sake –

Why can't I just fucking repress?

Like you're fucking supposed to?

But I actually think it's quite important –

To you know –

Think about it –

And weirdly –

It doesn't usually make me that upset –

Till I push it really fucking far –

I just think it's important –
You know –
That I try to understand –
Understand what this has done to me –
Cause it's fucked up –
It was year 6 –
That's concrete –
I know that to the two people I've told I implied I was
younger –
Just makes it sound better –
Doesn't it?
Well not better –
Obviously not better –
But more understandable –
I mean –
Fucking hell –
Am I saying that at 11 you could have been in control?
Are we actually saying –
Or am I actually saying that at that age you are too old to
have experienced genuine sexual assault –
I'm being melodramatic –
Aren't I?
Sorry –
What I mean is –
That at 11 –
At 11 I knew it was wrong –
I knew what those parts of my body were for –
God –
I knew what it fucking meant –
A bit –
I didn't tell my parents –
Cause I knew it was wrong –
So I try and deal with it alone –
It's best –
Isn't it?
But I get stuck –

It's difficult –
Well actually –
Probably impossible –
To consider the implications of things upon yourself –
If you get what I mean?
I can't think about me –
What's that word?
When you can't think about something and not think
about yourself?
OK –
Cause I can't think about myself –
From a distance –
You know?
I can only think about myself –
From myself.

I'm not making any sense.

So I get into all this weird shit –
When I try to think about it objectively.
Yes.
That's it.
Objectively.

Cause right –
This is what I've been thinking –
Maybe I'm actually supposed to be gay.
This is what I've been thinking.
Maybe –
Actually –
Deep down I'm gay.
But right –
When this all happened –
Cause of all the shame and everything –
I now think I'm straight because when I think of gayness
I think of that and that was bad.

Cause sometimes –
Right –
Sometimes –
I fucking hate women.
But then sometimes I fucking hate men.
I mean I fucking hate everyone.
It's not about that.

I think it right –
Cause I think that's why it happened in the first place.
Maybe he could tell –
Tell that I was confused –
So he got onto me –
I don't know if you can be confused when you're like –
What –
5?
OK –
I've got to stop lying.
12.
You can probably be confused at 12.
I mean surely if there is like a subconscience –
Subconscious –
Or whatever –
It would be there from always –
Right?
I mean –
I haven't read the books –
But it would be.
Deep down.
Fucking hell this is bull-shit isn't it?
Of course I'm not fucking gay.
I don't even know if I believe in all this 'deep down' shit –
Cause when I think about it –
This is what fucking happens.
I start talking about the fact that I'm probably actually gay –

But because of my first sexual experience I now want
to fuck women.
Fucking bull-shit.
Cause I do actually want to have sex with women –
And I do not want to have sex with men.
At least –
I don't think I want to have sex with men.
And now I'm back to the fucking beginning –

I like the idea of the 'deep down' though.
That depth.

I like to think –
Sometimes –
When I'm out –
With my mates –
Or just chatting to anyone –
When they are talking shite –
Most of the time –
I like to think that due to this thing –
I have this depth that they can't understand –
I like to think that this inexpressible thing has happened
to me –
That this horrible thing –
That everyone would fucking agree with me is horrible –
Has happened to me –
And all I would have to do is tell them and everything I'd
ever done would take on this new significance –
Everything I'd done would no longer be the action of some
dick –
But it would be the action of a person who was damaged.
But then who the fuck isn't damaged?

I just want someone –
Just anyone –
To look at me and tell me what is wrong with me.

Tell me what this has done to me.
Cause I think maybe nothing –
But what if it was everything?

It was my first sexual experience.
That's got to fuck with you.
Right?

STALKER:

Note for Male Performer:
The 'girl' spotted early in the piece becomes a 'boy'.

Example:
'I was waiting for a bus home and I saw this boy'.
'Natural markings of his body'.

I spend hours online looking at tattoos.
Like literally hours.
It gets to the point where I can't even count anymore cause it's just been so long.
I'm doing it while I do everything else.
Watching TV –
Cooking –
Working –
I don't even like them.
Like is a weird word –
Cause yes –
I don't like them –
But obviously there is something about them that I find absolutely fucking amazing –
Cause I'm always fucking looking at them.
I've never known mine.
See this is what I think –
I think you either know it –
Or you don't.

You've got to completely just get it –
Or what's the point?
I mean –
It's not like I'm saying some of us have this inner –
Innate symbol –
That completely one hundred per cent just is us –
But some people kind of get it –
You see their tattoo –
And you think –
Yeah –
I get you.
I never speak to them –
So I could be wrong.
But it seems like it.
So I just like looking at them.

By the way –
Before I continue –
I just really have to point out that I'm a hero.
Yeah.
I'm a hero.
Well –
That's what the BBC said.
When they interviewed me –
About me being a hero.
I'm sure you've all got it.

I was waiting for a bus home and I saw this girl –
At the stop.
Well –
First I noticed her tattoo.
And it was just lovely.
That's a stupid word.
Sorry.
I saw this tattoo –
It was just a line –

A black line around her wrist that kind of –
It's difficult to describe –
Marked out her veins and bones –
It followed the –
I dunno –
Natural markings of her body.
I was going to say –
There was something sensual about it –
But you probably already get it.

A bus arrived.
She got on.
So did I.

The bus was packed.
But I managed to sit next to her.
Probably looked creepy.
On the bus I just remember feeling so fucking aware of
every little movement I made.
Human bodies are so fucking noisy –
Breathing –
Swallowing –
Shifting leg positions –
She was so silent.
So I had to make myself more silent –
So I could listen.
I couldn't stop swallowing –
I must have been nervous.
Have you ever tried not swallowing when it's all building
in your mouth?
It's actually impossible.
Sorry.
I thought if I talked about the physical manifestations of
desire without actually mentioning any emotion I could get
away with it.
But it turns out you always sound like an arsehole –

So to hell with it.
I was so fucking excited.
I just felt so much potential that night.
I don't know what I wanted to happen –
But I could feel it –
At the pit of my stomach.

This is the bit I've told people a million times.
Here goes –
A man –
Wearing a knee-length green parka jacket –
With chin-length brown hair –
Walked upstairs.
I didn't actually see him walk up the stairs –
As I was already upstairs –
But considering that at some point he emerged upstairs –
He must have transferred his body from downstairs to
upstairs after boarding the bus –
And I assume he did this through the process of walking.
Sorry.
Police get very picky about exactly what you did and didn't
see.
He stood at the top of the stairs and looked around.
He walked down the aisle.
He didn't hold the bars even though the bus was moving.
I don't know how I remember it so clearly.
Maybe I'm inventing this crap to make him seem sinister –
When he seemed perfectly normal.
He probably did hold the bars.
This bit I'm quite clear on –
He pulled a baseball bat from somewhere under his coat.
People started to notice.
I don't remember any noise.
He then raised the bat above his head –
Brought it down –
Fast –
And whacked the guy sat in front of him full in the face.

He continued bringing the bat down.
Blood spurted everywhere.
The guy fell forward hitting his head on the bar in front of him.
There was then more blood.
Followed by screams.

I was so fucking excited.
This was massive.

He held the bat up again.
He was really close to me.
I stood up and stabbed him in the stomach with my keys.
He just stopped –
He fell –
And stopped.
Then we all sat back down and waited for the police.

I still have no fucking idea why I did that.
That was hands down the stupidest thing I've ever done.
I really didn't think at the time that this would be seen as
any different from what he did.
But everyone saw it as being very different –
People were crying.
I don't understand.
I was still fucking excited.

The police stuff was all very boring.

He didn't die –
By the way –
I didn't kill someone –
I realise that's a really vital part of the story.

And then it was on the news and I was this hero.
I'd saved a bus full of people.
Me.

The girl I got on the bus for.
She was fucking annoying when I spoke to her.
I was wrong about her tattoo giving her an innate
awareness.
That's still a great phrase though –
Innate awareness.

She gave me a present to say thank you –
They all fucking did.
She bought me a fucking cupcake.

I fucking hate cupcakes.

Cause –
Think about it –
Right –
They're supposed to be this new –
Like –
Friendly thing or whatever –
But they are literally the most antisocial thing.
Think about it.
If you wanted to be social –
You'd bake a cake and then you would share that cake.
A cake is inherently fucking social and a cupcake is
inherently fucking antisocial –
You buy the box as a group and then eat a fucking cupcake
all by your fucking self.
Oh look –
All of this icing is for me!!
The masses and masses of icing –
All for me!!
Why do they always have so much fucking icing?
Actually –
It makes me sick.
Why would anyone ever need that much icing?
I guess they're actually about indulgence –

Cause right now –
We all just need to indulge ourselves so much don't we?

I mean I indulge.
I am a hero after all.

NOBODY: Nothing happens to me –
Ever.
I'd go further than that.
I'd say that nothing has ever happened to me.
I can't tell you anything significant that has ever happened
to me.

I remember one night –
Late –
I was flicking through the TV –
And I paused on one channel –
There was some film –
Some serious film –
With some serious actor –
And he was watching porn –
He was watching porn and not wanking –
Just staring –
Seriously staring.
He was flicking through porn channels and just staring.
That scene.
I just looked –
And that was me.
I've watched a lot of TV.
I mean –
I watch a lot of TV.
But that scene –
That scene –
That would be me.
Out of any other moment I have ever witnessed –
That one sticks.
That is fundamentally depressing.

I think simply in the act of saying that I've condemned the
21st century
And that film was old.
That film was from the 20th century –
Would be way worse now.
This'll show you how old –
The film is partly set in the Twin Towers.
It has long shots of people moving through the
Twin Towers.
And you think that's crazy –
That's fucking crazy.
But in the end –
They are just two buildings.
It's just footage of two reasonably banal buildings.
I think the actor won an Oscar.
I guess it did get to me.

I went to university and graduated from university.
Maybe that's something –
But then loads of people go to university.
And every year more people go to university –
Most years anyway.
And you're supposed to go to university.
You go to school and then you go to university.

I haven't done anything that I wasn't ultimately expected to do.

I haven't even done a lot of the stuff other people have done.
I haven't been in love.
On that topic –
I haven't had good sex –
I haven't kissed someone and been excited by it.
I haven't been excited by anyone –
In that way –
Or in any other ways.
I haven't cum and called out someone's name.

I've never cum and felt like it was anything other than a
biological function.
I've never touched anyone and felt more than their skin.
I haven't masturbated over someone I know –
I haven't even masturbated over people –
Just detached sexual organs –
I mean –
They are attached –
But the whole body isn't in view.
I don't really masturbate that often anyway –
Just when it's unavoidable.
People say –
They say –
Get yourself out there!
Ask someone out!
Go on!
And I just think –
Who?
I can't imagine anyone I would ever consider asking out.

I have fantasies.
When I move about –
I think about stuff –
I plan things.
Moving to some distant land and writing about it –
And that writing being the best thing that's ever been
written –
Objectively.
Or I move to LA and make the best film of all time with no
budget –
And win all the Baftas.
Or I set up a publishing company in London that's really
fucking radical and starts some kind of movement –
Or I join a movement –
Go to Palestine –
Become a freedom fighter.

Ultimately I'm met with praise and glory and everyone
wants to fuck me and I fuck them all and it's great.
But these aren't ambitions –
Cause I finished university and didn't move to New York
and start a motorcycle gang.
I didn't even look up flights.
This didn't really bother me.
Maybe in the distant future I'll care –
I imagine being middle-aged and having nothing is worse
than having nothing now.

I walk around by myself –
With headphones –
I pick some melancholic album –
And I just wander –
Aimlessly –
Through busy streets –
Or whatever.
I just walk around and I think about things.
All kinds of things –
Not just concerned with myself –
Concerned with all manner of things.
Concerned with the whole world.
And I think this makes me a truly meaningful person.
I have depth.
And that's just great.

I don't feel I've experienced anger.
I have been angry –
But it was fleeting –
I got over it –
I've never experienced any kind of sustained anger.
There's that stereotype of the guy in anger-management –
The guy who can't control his anger.
Who just –
You know –

What's that phrase?
Sees red.

I have never been able to relate.
This is not an experience I understand.
I've thought about someone screaming at me –
Someone just fucking screaming at me –
All kinds of horrible –
Demeaning things.
He rips me to shreds –
Lays it out bare –
And I would cry –
And apologise –
And beg –
And beg for forgiveness.
And I –
I –

By the same author

Some People Talk About Violence
9781783199648